# How to Open a Mobile Catering Business

## Turn Your Passion for Food Into a Lucrative Line of Work

Jaylani Viotto

Please consult a licensed professional before attempting any techniques outlined in this book.

By reading this document, the reader agrees that under no circumstances is the author responsible for any losses, direct or indirect, that are incurred as a result of the use of information contained within this document, including, but not limited to, errors, omissions, or inaccuracies.

# Table of Contents

# Introduction

My guess is that you're passionate about food. If that's the case, it's great that you have a passion for something. The question is can you make money from your passion? Lots of people are passionate about lots of different things whether it be music, sports, or art, for example. Being able to make a living, and not just a living but a good living, off of something you love is an entirely different story. With this book though, I want you to be able to feel confident to know that you can pull this off and make it happen. I want you to feel convicted that if you put in the work, you truly can do this full-time and live well off of it. To get to that point though, it is going to take some sacrifice. No one can make the necessary sacrifices except for you. Without the right know-how, all of your sacrifices will be for nothing and that's what this book is here to change.

# Chapter 1: Is This Even Profitable and What Do You Need to Get Started

So to kick things off I want to talk about the strengths of what this business can offer to you and what type of supplies you'll need to get things going. As I mentioned in the introduction, having a passion is the first step but that doesn't guarantee you'll be successful. However, by being in the food business, there are some advantages that will naturally be on your side.

## People Have to Eat

What's the best part about being in the food business? Well, it's the fact that people have to eat to survive! Sure people don't have to eat food provided by you to survive, but they do have to eat something. And the interesting thing about food is that people can cook and prepare their own meals, but sometimes we need a break. As you know there's a lot of work that goes into buying, preparing, and cleaning to make a meal. There's also a lot of mental load that goes into thinking about what you want to eat. So a lot of times people will spend money to get fast food or to go to a restaurant and be served. People will do this even if the economy is bad and they don't have any money.

## Large Groups of People Have to Eat as Well

Even on a larger scale, people still have to eat, but now the problem is much bigger. It's a lot harder to feed a group of people than it is to feed yourself or your family. The mental load of preparing food to feed people for an event such as a corporate party or wedding is even bigger and more stressful. People expect to be fed at events like these and this is where you come into play. So all of this is to say that you're in a business that's essential but it is a luxury. Food is essential but catering is a luxury. Still, though, the market has shown time and time again that catering is a luxury people aren't willing to part ways with and it's hard to see that changing anytime in the future in good economies or bad. As long as you're able to get the exposure you need for your business, people will book with you. It's as simple as that. So if you're ever struggling, look at how you're marketing your company and how good your offer is. Chances are something is off with one of those things rather than the market being unwilling to pay you.

## People Will Always Want to Eat Delicious Food

So even though you're in an area of the food business that's considered a luxury, why do people keep coming back for more? Well, another reason is because people will always want delicious food. Yes, you have to eat, but you don't have to eat boring foods all of the time. If you're able to provide your guests with amazing and delicious foods, companies will hire you again. Friends will recommend you to their friends that are getting married. As we all know food and eating is so much more than just nourishing our bodies. It's an experience we enjoy doing and when there's a group of people, it can bring us together for a fun time socially.

## You Get to Be Around Food

A catering business gives you the opportunity to live out your passion of cooking and preparing meals. You're not dealing with a bunch of boring paperwork all of the time or anything like that. You actually get to be on your feet moving around and working with your hands to create something truly special that people will enjoy. The variety here is also endless because there are a ton of different options for the foods that you can feed people with.

## This Business is Definitely Profitable

With some businesses, it's hard to make a real profit, if any at all. You also have to invest a bunch of upfront capital and wait for years before you make a profit. You also have to quit your current job and dive all in if you want a shot at being successful. With a mobile catering business, yes, you are going to have to invest some money upfront, but you can quickly make that money back and make a profit very quickly. You also don't have to quit your job right now if you have a family to feed. This is something you can do in your spare time to prepare for the event. Depending on what niche you decide to go with, most of the events you cater for will likely be on the weekends anyways, which will be a seamless fit if you're working a job Monday-Friday.

# What Supplies Will You Need?

When it comes to supplies, there are certain things you know you'll need, and then there are things you know you'll need, but it will be best to hold off on purchasing them. For example, every event is going to need plates and utensils, but it's a good idea to hold off on these until you know the type of event you're catering for. Paper plates may be acceptable or they may not be depending on the event you're catering for. Some will be fancier than others, but some of your supplies will be the same regardless.

## Utensils (Forks, Spoons Knives), Plates, Napkins, and Cups

These are essential items that you'll need at every event, but as I just mentioned, it's not a bad idea to hold off on buying these until you get your first deposit. This way you'll know the type of event you're catering for, and you can buy the appropriate type of utensils, plates, and cups. If you're the type of person who likes to be prepared well in advance, then go ahead and buy some plastic forks, spoons, and knives as well as some paper plates and styrofoam cups. This way you will be prepared for a general event that could come up at a moment's notice.

## Serving Utensils

There are a variety of serving utensils that you'll need depending on what kind of foods you'll be serving. It's best to get the basic necessities so that way you are prepared for anything that comes your way. So be sure you have multiple tongs, spatulas, and cradles on hand for any event that you cater for. It's always best to have a backup just in case. Your tongs might fall on the ground, and it's super handy to be able to grab another pair and continue to move forward. You could have to call in for backup, and you'll need to have the extra supplies ready for someone else to be able to come in and lend an extra hand.

## To-Go Boxes

To-go boxes aren't something that a catering company will always supply. Generally speaking, people eat what they are served, they'll eat what they want, and the leftovers on the plate will go to waste more times than not. Why not make a reputation for your company to be known for going above and beyond? Be the catering company that's thoughtful and thinks about the customer enough to bring to-go boxes. It's a small little thing that can go a long way. Yes, you're trying to impress the company or people who hired you, but you're also trying to impress the guests. You don't know what type of connections they have, what they do for work, if they're engaged, or anything else. When you're serving the guests, you are auditioning your services to them and they just might hire you for an event they have coming up, so every small detail matters.

## Fold-Out Tables

Having tables is an absolute must. Purchasing fold-out tables is the best way to go about things because they're the easiest to transport. You're going to need portable tables to place your food on when you're serving the guests. You're also going to need a table or two for all of the drinks so people can just walk by grab a drink and go. The number of tables that you'll need will vary depending on the size of the event that you're doing. It's not a bad idea to purchase 4 fold-out tables as this will be enough to cover a variety of different events for you. And in the case that you need 6 tables for an event, you can always go out and buy two more, or possibly even rent or borrow them, if that size of an event is a rare occurrence for you.

## Food-Handling Gloves

Another key aspect to looking like a clean professional who cares about the work they do and not getting people sick is to wear food-handling gloves. Some people might not think anything of you not wearing gloves, but others will notice and you don't want to come across as neglectful with any catering job that you do. You can buy nitrile or poly plastic gloves, whatever suits your preference. The one thing you want to make sure of is that they are powder-free because no one wants powder on their chicken, for example. It will certainly freak a bunch of people out.

## Tablecloths

Are tablecloths an essential that you have to have? No, you can get by without them. Again though, we need to have the mindset that every detail big or small matters. This attention to detail is what will separate you from your competitors and make you look like an experienced professional even if you're just getting things started. You'll use the tablecloths to put over your fold-out tables to make your food look more presentable. In terms of what color you should get, I recommend going with black. Black will be a versatile color for a wide range of events and it will hide stains much better than white. You're serving food and drinks, so it's easy for a guest to knock over a cup or for food stains and crumbs to get on your tablecloth while serving. You, of course, may find yourself doing an event where a different color may be more appropriate. One example could be serving a company whose brand colors are mostly red. In that case, it wouldn't be a bad idea to buy a red tablecloth specifically for this event because, again, attention to detail is what matters here. What you don't want to do is buy every color under the sun because most of those colors will rarely, if ever, be used.

## Chafing Dishes

These dishes are what you're going to be serving your food from. They'll have burners underneath them so that the food will stay warm and ready to serve. You'll want to start out with at least two of these, and then you can buy more once you're taking on an event that's big enough to require more chafing dishes.

## Cooler

Nobody wants to drink a warm beverage, especially if you're serving in a warm climate. You're going to need to bring ice and have a way to prevent it from melting before you make your drinks. A cooler is a cheap way to go about doing this and you can get something basic. You don't need something that will maintain ice for days, after all, you really only need something that can store ice for the day. A $30-$50 cooler will work just fine, you don't need to go out and buy a $300 cooler. I would recommend buying a smaller size and a larger size to help provide coverage for any event that you do. During smaller events, it will be much easier to lug around a smaller cooler if the bigger one isn't needed.

## Drink Dispenser

You'll need something to transport your liquids in. For example, if you're serving sweet and unsweetened tea for your beverages, it can save space to have all of the tea contained in one 5 or 10-gallon container and transport things that way so long as it's secure. Some of the fancier drink dispensers don't have a way to properly seal the top, so it wouldn't be practical to use for transportation. In some cases though, such as tea, you could buy it by the gallon and transport it that way. Then you can pour the tea equally into cups and set them out on one of your fold-out tables. The other way you can go about things is to set up your drink dispenser and have guests pour out their own drinks. Regardless, a drink dispenser helps give you a lot of versatility and it can help you save time so it's a worthy investment.

## Food Warmer and Refrigerator

You're going to need to prep your food in advance before the event. Once the food is prepped, you're going to need a commercial refrigerator to store all of the food in and a food warmer once it's time to start getting the food ready for the event. These may not be necessary items though if you're working out of a commercial kitchen that has additional refrigeration that you can store your food in until the event date arrives.

# Chapter 2: What To Do Before You Get Paying Clients

We'd all like to start a business and get paid right away, but that's not how things work. There are a few things you need to think about before you take on your first paying client. By taking care of these things first, you'll best prepare yourself for success.

## Forming Your Business Entity

When you work for someone as an employee, business entities aren't something you have to think about. You show up, do your job, and get paid. Things are a bit different than that when it comes to starting a business. You need to think about how you want to set up your business. It's easier to plan this out when you're starting rather than to deal with it later on. So what are your options? Well, you have a sole proprietorship, an LLC, or a corporation. There are two types of corporations, a C corporation and an S corporation. Corporations are mostly for bigger businesses that will involve investors and the intent to go public one day. Due to things such as double taxation with a C corporation, this likely isn't going to be the best avenue for you to start out with. What I recommend is forming an LLC. This entity will establish your business as an actual business, and that may not seem like a big deal, but it is. Sole proprietorships are not viewed as separate entities, which means that any potential liability falls directly on you. By having your business separated from yourself, you help create protections on your personal assets. It's important though that you actually act like a business should act. You don't want to form an LLC only to act like a sole proprietorship. In these instances, something can happen known as piercing the corporate veil, which essentially would put your assets at risk in the event of a lawsuit. So what are some things you can do to look like an actual operating business? The first thing you want to do is set up your own business bank account. There are plenty of good options out there. You can set up a new account with a traditional bank or even an online bank. In the world of catering, it's rare that you'll ever get paid in cash, so online banking isn't a bad option to consider. Here are a few banks I recommend looking into:

- Lili
- Bluevine
- Novo

- Grasshopper
- Relay

Each bank will have its own pros and cons. You need to decide what matters most to you and choose based on that. Some banks have lower limits when it comes to the amount of money you can transfer per month. Some banks offer a higher APY than others. Some will offer the ability to have separate accounts, while others won't. So it's important to do your research on these things to figure out what you want to prioritize. The other thing you want to do is hold a meeting at least once per year. Yes, even if you are the only person in your company, you still want to hold a meeting with yourself and document what you covered. If you thought about new plans for marketing or how you want to change your pricing, then log these things as well as when the meeting started and ended. The easiest way to do this is to search for a meeting template online and follow it. Lastly, if you've never formed a business before, the idea of it can certainly seem overwhelming and expensive. The good news is that it doesn't have to be complicated as there are plenty of companies that specialize in this very thing. All you have to do is fill out some basic information about your company and they'll take care of the rest. The process is pretty streamlined, which is great if you would otherwise have no clue where to begin. Here are a few websites to check out that can help with the formation of your LLC:

- Legal Zoom
- Bizee
- Tailor Brands

The amount it will cost to form your LLC will vary depending on the state that you live in, so be mindful of that and do some research ahead of time so that you're aware of what the cost will be to file.

## Do You Need Insurance as a Catering Company?

We live in a crazy and unpredictable world, so it's best to get insurance to help with coverage for those what-if moments. Additionally, some corporations may require proof of insurance before they hire you to cater for them, so insurance is helpful for more than just the coverage it provides. There are a few different types of insurance that you'll want to look into. The first probably won't be applicable to you right away and that's workers' compensation insurance. You're not going to need this type of insurance if you don't have any employees, but it can help to cover expenses related to an employee getting hurt on the job and help to cover wages the worker would be missing out on due to an injury they sustained on the job. Another type of insurance that could be worth looking into would be commercial property insurance. This can help to cover the expenses for replacing your equipment if it was damaged. Let's say you're working outdoors on a windy day and the wind blows some of your equipment off the table and breaks it. Additionally, it can also cover missed wages due to your equipment being broken. So if you were unable to complete the job because the wind ruined your equipment, then it's possible to recoup the missed earnings. Generally, though, most of the equipment isn't going to be that expensive to replace on your own, so this is something worth looking into, but it's not a necessity by any means. The last type of insurance is general liability insurance, and this will help to cover general things that can happen with your business. Think of this like a blanket policy that can help provide coverage for a variety of different accidents that could happen due to the line of work that you're in.

## Food Handler and Preparation Certification

Is this certification a requirement in your state? Well, it may or may not be, but it's still a great idea to obtain not just for yourself, but for anyone you hire in the future. The reason why it's a good idea regardless is because it's not expensive and it doesn't take long to complete. You'll enhance your knowledge of how to keep your food sanitary to help prevent people from getting sick, and it's a good look for your company. You'll be prepared in case someone wants to see this certification before hiring you, and even if it's not asked for, you can use it to help close a deal to show that you take every event very seriously.

## What Additional Licenses and Permits Will You Need?

Aside from taking care of the things I've mentioned in the chapter thus far, are there any other licenses or permits that you need to acquire before you go ahead and get started? Well, that's difficult to say because each state will be different on if something such as a business license is a requirement or if you need to get a permit before you're allowed to cater at a certain event. Even within your own state, different counties can have different regulations for what is and isn't required of you. The best way to go about things is to go to the Secretary of State website for the state that you reside in. This is where you can learn more information and ask questions that you have. Then it's also a good idea to contact your city and ask questions as well to ensure you're covering your basis.

## Where Will You Work From?

There's another aspect you have to consider here and that's where are you going to be preparing the food from? Well, the answer to that will once again depend on circumstances. Where you live, what type of foods you're preparing, and how much money your business makes all can play a factor in where you're allowed to operate. It comes down to something known as cottage food laws. These are laws that will allow you to prepare foods for sale from your home so long as certain requirements are met. One example in some places is if your gross sales are less than $50,000 per year and you're only selling foods that don't require refrigeration. These requirements will vary from state to state, so it's best to do some research and see what you can find about your state. In the majority of cases though, you won't be able to operate from your own home, and that's totally okay. You don't have to settle for an alternative being having to sign a lease on your own kitchen space. Instead, you can simply rent a commercial kitchen as needed and prepare your food that way. This will give you the benefit of being able to prepare food without having to take on the extra stress of dealing with things like health inspections. The commercial kitchen will just be there ready for you to use when you need it. This will allow you to save money, especially in the beginning.

# Chapter 3: Who Do You Want to Serve?

Another key aspect to being successful in this business that not a lot of people in this business think about is what type of client they would ideally like to serve. Right now, you might be thinking that you'll take on anyone that you can get and that's not a bad mentality to have. You want to niche down though for a couple of reasons. The first reason has to do with how you promote your company. If you try to appeal to everyone, you appeal to no one. The strategies you employ and the wording of your marketing materials will all vary depending on who it is that you'd ideally like to serve. If you're just trying to serve anyone who would pay, then you will ironically have a tougher time getting paying clients. You'll subtly come across as more desperate without even realizing it, and you're not speaking to anyone. When you're able to speak to someone's direct pain points, they'll raise their hand and say that's me. That's when your phone, email, and DMs will start blowing up. The pain point of someone trying to cater a meal for their company event is different from someone planning to feed guests at their wedding. When you niche down, you're able to continually understand the pain points of your ideal clientele better and better. This further strengthens your marketing messages and creates a snowball effect. None of this can happen though if you're unable to take that first plunge of choosing an ideal client in the first place. Yes, the idea of this is scary, but it will be less daunting by the end of this chapter.

## What Different Kinds of Clients Are Out There?

In the catering world, there's no shortage of options when it comes to the kind of people that you can serve. Here are a few examples to give you some ideas:

- Corporations
- Weddings
- Conferences
- Events
- Family Gatherings/Reunions
- Baby Showers
- Retirement Parties
- Birthday Parties
- Engagement Parties

Of course, it's not about picking one of these things and sticking to that. Some of these ideas are similar and would go together such as weddings and engagement parties. Naturally, if you catered for someone's engagement party, it would go hand-in-hand to cater for their wedding as you're still serving the same target client. What I am saying though is that serving someone for a wedding is different from a corporate party, which is different from serving people who are at a car convention. So how do you go about deciding who is your ideal client that you'd like to serve?

## Choosing Your Ideal Client

When it comes to picking a niche, it can be easy to say, "Oh this would be the most profitable, so I'm going to go with that." That's not a bad line of thinking, however, it's important to zoom out and look at the entire picture. Sure, let's say for the sake of an example that focusing on corporations could bring you in more money than engaged couples. Well, if something is more profitable, then that likely means there's more competition. With more competition, you're going to have to work that much harder to stand out to earn business. If your heart isn't fulfilled by serving this type of client due to the stress or the fact that you might like working with a different niche more, then you're going to get burnt out. All of the extra effort you're putting into the business isn't going to feel like it's worth it. So instead of trying to chase the dollar, start out by thinking about which type of client excites you the most. Which clientele would have you the most eager to work for? That's the main thing that you should think about when choosing a niche. Worst case scenario if you are too lasered in with your niche, you can always change it or broaden it. There's nothing making you stick to what you originally chose. For example, maybe you recently got married and because of that you can relate to someone who would be planning a wedding, and you'd love nothing more than to work with someone to help ease the burden when it comes to the food portion of wedding planning. You'd also have relevant and relatable experience so you'd have a direct understanding of the pain points of this client and you can speak directly to that with your marketing materials. It could be the case that you've worked at a company before where you were in charge of coordinating the catering for company pirates and events, and you remember how stressful it was trying to please everyone. If you feel like you could help take the edge off of the situation by providing a variety of unique food options, you can speak to that when promoting, and your material will stand out to someone like I just described.

## What Are the Characteristics of Your Ideal Client?

Once you've chosen the ideal client you'd like to serve, it's important to spend some time thinking about their characteristics. Here are some ideas of things that you should think about:

- What do they search for online?
- What types of accounts do they follow on social media?
- What position at a company is typically responsible for handling catering (hint-hint secretary or assistant) and what are some of the stressors of their job?
- What are the pain points of this person? For example, what are some things a bride would be stressing over when planning for her wedding?
- What do they like to do in their leisurely time?
- Where do they like to spend their money?
- Do they like luxury or just the basics?

- What's their preferred way to communicate (text, DM, email, phone call, in person)?
- What kind of lifestyle do they live?
- What are they looking to gain from your service (just to be fed, look good for their boss, really wow the guests)?
- Is the company very corporate-like or more laid back?

The above list isn't supposed to be an end-all-be-all, but it is meant to help give you a jumpstart. Once you go through and think about these questions and any others you come up with, it's now time to move to the next step.

## Creating Your Ideal Client Profile

You want to spend some time thinking about and answering the above questions to help you create a client avatar. Essentially, you can picture this exact type of person any time you're creating marketing materials or trying to close a deal. Here's an example of what this might look like. In this case, our ideal client is a bride planning out her wedding:

"Sally is in her late 20s or early 30s and is having a stressful time planning out her wedding. She wants everything to be just right for her special day and she wants things to be seamless and easy because there is a lot going on. Unfortunately, she isn't getting much help planning from her fiancé. She does have a budget, but she's willing to pay for someone else to make her life easier. When she's not at her 9-5 job or planning for her wedding, she enjoys spending her free time scrolling through social media after a long day of work, getting brunch with her friends, shopping on a Saturday afternoon, or watching her favorite streaming services."

## Now What?

Once you've put together a client profile, what should you do with it? Well, you'll want to keep it in mind for any type of marketing material that you produce. You also want to keep these characteristics in mind whenever you're trying to close someone to book with you. You may not know the exact pain points of your ideal clientele yet, and that's okay. As time goes on and you start to work with more and more people, you'll start to learn more about them. You'll be able to tell what details they're specifically looking for to help put their mind at ease. After you work with them you can also send them an email and ask questions to get feedback about your business. Some of those questions can be, why did you choose to work with me and what could have made your experience better? These questions will help to give you better insight into what your ideal type of client is looking for. So when you're creating your initial profile, don't stress over making it perfect. Instead, do the best you can with the information you have and work towards improving it as time goes on. With your ideal profile, you'll now be able to have this in your back pocket for any ad you run, any post you make on social media, or any other marketing material for that matter. For example, if you know that a lot of your customers are brides who don't tend to get a lot of help when it comes to planning, then you can speak directly to them to help compel people to take action. Here's an example of what an ad campaign could look like because you took the time to think about the biggest pain points your clients experience:

"Are you stressed to the max right now planning your wedding? Is it even more stressful because you're not getting help from your significant other? One of the biggest stressors to planning is catering because figuring out what to feed everyone and how much food you'll need is a lot to think about. I'm here to take the catering burden off of your shoulders because I've been in your shoes before and I get it. My goal is to make the catering aspect of your wedding planning something you enjoy, not something that makes you want to pull your hair out. I make it seamless to determine the best foods to feed everyone and how to pull it off without a hitch. If you'd like more information, click the link below to book a free consultation."

# Chapter 4: Charge Per Plate

This chapter is going to be discussing pricing. If you've never run your own business before, then you're not used to coming up with your own pricing. There is a lot of variance within coming up with your own pricing. For example, if you were running your own e-commerce store, you'd buy products at a certain price point, and then sell them at a 30-50% markup. People will then come to your website, see your pricing and then decide if they want to buy or not. With catering it's a lot different. You want to be able to list your prices on your website because things will be different for each client. You'll have to work with them to understand their needs before you're able to give them a quote. And this is where things can quickly go south. Lack of experience plus having to develop unique pricing for each client can cause people to short-change themselves if they aren't confident in what they're bringing to the table. If this was a book about e-commerce, I could easily tell you to sell at 30-50% more than you buy for and that would be that. Given the nuisance of pricing in the catering world, we certainly have more details to dive into.

## Please Don't Do This

As the title of this chapter suggests, you'll want to charge per plate when it comes to catering. Sadly though, many people who are new to the catering scene will not do this. Instead, they'll charge for the cost of materials plus labor. The labor they'll factor in won't even be that much. Even worse yet, they'll share a price breakdown of how much each different thing costs with the client. In theory, this seems like a good idea. It feels comfortable because you shouldn't have to worry about the customer balking at your price if you're able to show a breakdown of how you arrived at the price in the first place. Doing this though really shows a lack of confidence in your pricing. It's as if you have to show a breakdown of your pricing to try and prove to the customer that you're not trying to overcharge them. And this brings up a whole separate point. Maybe you didn't grow up with a lot of money. It was scarce and so you always had a negative relationship with money. Now that you're running a business, you feel as if you're taking money from someone else and so you only want the least amount possible so you can complete the job. Well doing that is going to make you miserable and leave you wishing you never started this business in the first place. However, the main issue with giving the customer a breakdown of your prices is that it leaves you susceptible to being nitpicked and challenged on why you're charging this price for x,y, and z. You're essentially going to be spending a lot of time on this just to have to spend even more time adjusting things. Let's say you put on your price breakdown sheet that it's going to cost $60 for utensils. The customer might ask why it's going to cost that much for utensils. They'll ask where you're buying them from and then try to suggest a cheaper place. You're going to be doing a bunch of shopping around to try and get the best price to please the customer and this isn't a good use of your time. And this can happen for multiple different items on your list. Then the customer isn't going to understand why labor costs as much as it does and they'll try to get you to come down on your labor costs as well. What this all boils down to is that when your prices are cheap and you give a breakdown of why you're charging what you are, you tend to attract clients that will nickel and dime you. They'll try to squeeze you for everything they can, and it isn't worth the headaches that these clients can bring! Seriously, after dealing with people like this time and time again it will make you start to question if this business is something worth doing. I get that it can be a little intimidating if you've never done this before, but the biggest key to being successful with your pricing is to act with confidence. Even if you aren't confident with what you're doing or the price you're charging, go ahead and act confidently anyways. Practice your pricing over and over again in the mirror paying attention to your tone and body language until it becomes second nature. This way when it comes time to go over your prices with someone, you won't sound shaky. As soon as the customer senses hesitation, they'll either try and pounce on it or they'll go with someone else, even if their prices are higher. They'll do this because they can't trust you to get the job done and it's all due to a lack of confidence.

## Determining Your Price Per Plate

So, the correct way to go about things is to charge per plate and to not share your breakdown of how you arrived at that price point with the client. You see, it doesn't matter what type of client you're dealing with. It could be a company, a couple that's getting married, or whoever else, people know that catering isn't cheap. People know it's going to cost a good amount of money to feed a bunch of people. So it's okay to charge your worth and you'll get it when you approach with certainty and you only tell the customer the price per plate. Think about it, when you go anywhere all you see is the final price in most cases. Rarely do you ever see a price breakdown and it's for the same reasons that I've already discussed. So when it comes to your price per plate, what are some of the factors you need to think about in order to determine how much it's going to cost you to serve everyone? Well, there are a few things you need to think about. It all starts with the number of people that need to be fed and what you're feeding them. You can then work backwards from there. Now there are going to be some costs that will stay the same per person regardless of what's being served. For example, your utensil, napkin, cup, and beverage costs will be the same price per person just about every time, unless a fancier event calls for something you don't typically use. So this is something you could predetermine with a good degree of accuracy. Aside from utensil and food costs you also need to think about labor costs. Is this job going to require you to bring on additional help? Even if you're able to complete the job by yourself, you still want to charge for labor. In terms of how much you should be charging for this, think about how much profit (not gross income) you want to make from this job. It will all vary depending on the size of the event, but a good range to aim for is between $600-$1,200 in profit per event. Once you determine how much profit you'd like to make, you can then continue to work backwards to figure out your price per plate. For example, let's say the event you're doing is for 100 people. You figure out that it's going to cost you $10 to serve each person. If you charge $15 per plate, that will result in $500 of profit. If you charge $18 per plate, you will walk away with $800 in profit. Based on the amount of profit that you want to make, you can now give a solid price to the customer. So to finish out this example, let's say you determine that $800 in profit would be worth your time. You can now give a quote that it's going to cost $18 per plate. Now the customer knows the total price is going to be $1,800 to feed everyone. Generally speaking, you should end up charging around $15-$20 per plate. This will vary if you're catering for something more upscale that's going to require more expensive food options, additional labor, and fancier utensils. But typically when you're pricing things out if you land in that $15-$20 per plate area, then you can feel confident to move forward with that pricing.

# Chapter 5: How to Get Your Phone Ringing With Eager Customers

Throughout this book we've covered a good basis for what you need to do to get things off the ground and be successful in regards to your pricing. None of that info will matter if you're unable to get your business in front of potential clients who would be interested in your services. This chapter is going to help you fix that feeling of hopelessness when no one is reaching out to you. It's a defeating feeling and it can make you doubt your business altogether. There are a few different strategies I'm going to cover, but please know that this isn't some end-all-be-all when it comes to marketing your business. There are plenty of different ways in which you can gain exposure for your company, and some methods are more effective than others. That's why I want to focus on the most effective methods so that you don't waste any time.

## Pay to Be Featured on Food or Wedding Websites and Social Media Pages

There are plenty of big-name food and wedding blogs on the internet and that's good news for you. You don't even have to settle for print media as you could look for a podcast sponsorship as well. These websites and pages also come in a variety of sizes, which is good as well. The bigger the audience is on a given platform, the more expensive it will be for your company to be promoted on it. So it's not necessarily about paying for the biggest blog or podcast that you can find. It's about promoting yourself on a platform that's within your budget and that contains your target audience. This is where creating the client avatar comes into play. By knowing what type of content your ideal customer follows, you can best ensure that you're paying to be put directly in front of the people you want to see your message. An obvious example is to pay to be featured on a website that's all about weddings. People who are engaged will follow these blogs and they're the perfect type of person you want to see your promotion. What I recommend that you do is spend some time researching some different social media pages, website blogs, and podcasts and come up with a list of the ones that you'd like to reach out to. What you say when you reach out to these people isn't that important. All that really matters is that you have the money that they're asking for in exchange for the promotion. So ask around and get some different prices, and go with multiple different platforms that are within your budget. It's a good idea to diversify your budget across multiple different pages rather than to pour it all into one website or podcast, for example. By splitting things up, you'll be able to track and see which channel brought you the best return on your investment, and you can continue to pour more into what's working and less into what isn't working. The way that you can track the success of each campaign is by offering a unique promo code for each different channel that you're using. So if you run a paid promotion on two blogs, 2 social media pages, and 2 podcasts, then you'd want to come up with 6 different promo codes. Then whenever someone books with you and uses the code "podcast10" you'll know exactly which promotion created the sale.

## Cold Outreach to Businesses

You could be in a situation where you don't have a lot of spare money to invest in paid promotions. If that's the boat you find yourself in, don't worry, as there are free avenues that you can take advantage of. This is the case regardless of what type of client it is that you're trying to serve. For instance, if your main clientele are corporations, then you can send cold emails or cold call these companies to promote your services. What about if you're looking to serve people at weddings? Again this isn't an issue. You can go to wedding social media pages and look at the people who are liking the post. You can message the people who like and comment on the page's various posts to help promote your services. You can even just look at the followers of the account and message people that way. And since there are plenty of businesses that exist and tons of people who are on social media, there is no shortage of people that you can reach out to. There's a chance you don't feel comfortable with the thought of cold outreach and I can understand where you're coming from. The bottom line though is that you must get sales for your business to succeed. The great thing about cold outreach is that it's all up to you. You control how much of it you do and that can directly lead to your success. If you're not getting the type of response that you want, you can always message more people or change up what you're saying. The best part is that it's free so there really is no excuse if you want it badly enough. If you're intimidated by the thought of having to call companies, don't be. You're typically going to be talking to a secretary who isn't going to be rude to you, and you don't have to cold call if you don't want to. There's always email, so there are multiple ways to go about this. Just like with promoting your company on a podcast or blog, get started by creating a list of companies that you'd like to reach out to. Once you have your list, go ahead and contact the companies on the list and keep track of the date from when you reached out. This is important to do so that way you'll know when to follow up with them if you don't get an initial response back. So what should you say in your initial email? Something such as the following will be effective:

"Hello my name is Naomi from Naomi's catering. I'm reaching out because I'm currently offering a 10% discount on my service for the upcoming Labor Day weekend. My rates are very competitive and I do all of the thinking so you don't have to! If your company is interested in learning more information please do not hesitate to reply to this email or visit my website linked below. I hope you have a wonderful rest of your day!"

As you can tell, the email isn't very long and it doesn't need to be. People are either going to be interested or they won't be. People are also very busy so you can't expect them to read paragraphs and paragraphs about a business they know nothing about. You want to keep things to the point and focus on the benefits that you can provide to them. To put it bluntly, people don't care about your business, but they do care about solving a problem that they're experiencing. So if you come in and offer a solution, you can land the business. That's why the email focuses on offering a discount and talks about how the guesswork can be taken out of the equation to help make things simple. It is important to include some reason for why you're reaching out, such as an upcoming holiday or whatever the case may be. This makes it appear less random for why you're reaching out. Again though, you can take this and email multiple different companies to your heart's content, and remember this is a numbers game so don't beat yourself up if you send 3 emails and don't get a response from anyone.

## What About Individuals?

What if you're not trying to target businesses and instead you want to focus more on people, such as engaged couples? How do you go about this? As I mentioned a short time ago, you want to go to social media and look for accounts where your target audience is going to be. So if you're looking for people who are getting married, then go to pages that are about weddings. This is where you'll have the highest likelihood of coming across people who are in need of your services. The cool thing about social media is that the accounts you find will make posts and people will comment and like these posts. These are the people you want to reach out to first. The reason being is that you know these people are active on social media and give you the best chance at receiving a response. If the account doesn't have super high engagement, you can still turn to the followers of that account and message people that way. So what should you send to people? Well, you really want to cater to the platform that you're on. In the world of DMing, it's not about sending a big block of text. Rather it's better to break things up into chunks and ask questions to really understand the needs of the person you're talking to. So for instance, if you notice on someone's profile that they are engaged, you can send them a DM asking them if they have a caterer booked for their wedding yet. If they respond and say that they don't, you can now start to collect more information, just like you would with anyone else who shows interest in your services. Ask them roughly how many guests are going to be there, what type of food they're looking to serve, etc. You can continue to ask questions like this all the way to the point of sending them a link to collect a deposit. It all starts with a simple question and not trying to go all in right away. Just like with sending emails, you can do this as much as you want to help drive sales for your business.

## Attend Bridal Shows

There are trade shows for plenty of different things out there, and one such type of show is a bridal show. At these events, engaged couples will come and look at what the various vendors have to offer. Various types of vendors will be at these events, such as wedding venues, photographers, and of course people need to eat so you can cash in on this as a caterer as well. The awesome thing about attending a bridal show is that you're putting yourself in front of your target audience. It wouldn't make sense for people to show up if they weren't going to be getting married. However, just because you're in front of your target audience, that doesn't mean anything. You have to be able to seize the moment. Some people might be there early on in the process and they might causally be looking around. It's your job to help create urgency to help get them to book with you or at the very least, get their contact information so that you can follow up with them once it's closer to time for them to make a decision. Some couples will be early on in the process, so they might not be ready to commit now. Even with that being the case, you still need to be ready. At a bare minimum, make sure that you collect an email address so that you can follow up with them. However, you do want to try and seize the moment. The way that you can do this is by offering a discount for signing up at the event. You also want to bring flyers that have your company's information on them, and even go as far as bringing samples to really help people experience how amazing your food is in person. This is what will really separate you and make people want to sign up with you on the spot.

## Take Advantage of the Modern Age

I'd be remiss to not talk about social media considering how many people are on social media nowadays. People expect companies to have social media pages and you're going to be missing out in the long run if you don't have any social media accounts for your business. There really is a sea of different kinds of content that you can post when it comes to catering. Here are some ideas to help get your creative juices flowing:

- What are some of the challenges of being in the catering business?
- What steps do you take to ensure that the utmost care is given?
- What challenges come with serving so many people at once?
- Nightmare scenarios you were in and how you overcame them
- What is your favorite kind of food to serve and why
- What type of events you enjoy doing the most
- How you would prepare for a larger event vs a smaller one
- What made you want to become a caterer
- Post pictures and videos of you making the food
- Pictures of the various food that you make

-   What a sample plate would look like

## Don't Be Afraid to Do It for Free

If there are situations where you can cater a small event for free, you should consider doing so if you're struggling to generate leads. The idea of working for free probably doesn't sound too appealing to you, but you're really not working for free. You're working in exchange to promote your business. Let's say for example, some of your friends are gathering to watch a sporting event. You could offer to cook for the event. You don't necessarily have to pay for the food if others are willing to chip in. Then your food will do the talking. Now whenever your friends or your friends' friends are in need of a caterer, you'll be at the top of their minds. You can do this for any event that you'd have access to because of your network. It will help to get the ball rolling in terms of word of mouth.

# Chapter 6: What About Jobs that Are Too Big for Yourself?

In the catering business, you could book a customer that is too big for you to serve by yourself. The thing is that this could be your very first customer too, which means you always have to be prepared to bring on an extra set of hands if need be. This can be a bit tricky to navigate though. How do you find the right person and know that they can do a good job? What if you only need them sporadically and not on a consistent basis? These are some of the waters you're going to have to navigate. What you don't want to do is turn down a job because it's outside of your capacity to do the job by yourself. You're leaving money on the table at that point, and that's something I don't want you to have to do. It's better to be prepared so you can strike while the opportunity is hot.

## Should You Hire a Full-Time or Part-Time Employee?

The nature of this business can be a bit tricky. You could have 5 jobs in a row that you can complete by yourself, and then the 6th job requires an additional set of hands. If you make a hire, you're likely going to be paying this person for nothing most of the time, and that's not a good way to operate your business. So the solution to this problem isn't to hire a full-time or part-time employee. Instead, you need to look to bring in help on an as-needed basis. You'll essentially be looking to pay someone as a contractor. This will give your business the ultimate amount of flexibility, which you need, and it can also help produce some nice income on the side for someone who's already working a 9-5.

## What Questions Should You Ask?

Luckily, serving food and helping with set up and take down doesn't require a lot of skill. Even though that's the case, you still want to do your proper due diligence to ensure you're bringing on someone who will make your life easier and not harder. You don't want to butt heads with someone all of the time, it'll just make you wish that you were doing everything by yourself. So what are some questions you can ask the person to know if they'll be a good fit to work with you or not?

- Have you ever worked at a catering event before, and if so, how big was the event?
- Have you ever been in a customer service role before?
- How would you handle a guest approaching you and wanting seconds?
- How would you approach a guest asking you for a double serving of meat?

I like these questions because they pertain directly to what you'll be doing. If the person has previous experience working catering events, then that's a big plus. They'll understand the inner workings of how to get the job done. You'll still need to teach them to do things the way you want them to, but they'll definitely have a head start. If they don't have any direct experience, that's totally okay. That doesn't mean they'll be a bad fit for the job. It's still a good idea to ask them if they've worked in customer service before, as this is a relatable experience. Lastly, don't forget about specific scenario-based questions. You want to ask some of these questions because you want someone to think how you think. You're not going to be able to train someone for every specific situation that comes up, but if someone thinks like you do, then you can trust them to make the right choice if you're unavailable.

## Consider Doing This as Well

Asking questions is great and all, but if you're able to meet up with them in person and take them through a practice run, this would be even better. Have them practice serving plates, carrying the food, setting up the beverages, or whatever else you think you need to see them do before they're working with you on a real job. Go ahead and pay them for their time of course, and this will be well worth the investment on your end. You'll get to see potential mistakes that you can correct and you'll get a better understanding of how they'll work all before it's the real deal.

## How Much Should You Pay?

How much you pay someone is ultimately up to you, so long as you're paying people at least minimum wage. This however doesn't mean that you should offer minimum wage, but it will depend on a few factors. The first thing is how good is the person that you're looking to bring on. If they have previous experience with catering events and they think like you do, then that is more valuable than someone without experience. So you should look to pay someone more if they're a better fit. This will help to keep them around and make it less likely for them to leave. The location of your business will ultimately be the biggest determining factor for how much you pay someone. If you live in a rural area, you might pay someone $12-$13 an hour. If you live in a metropolitan area, you will be paying more possibly up to $18-$20 per hour. If you need something to look at as a basis for what you should pay, look and see what fast food restaurants are paying per hour in your area. This will give you a good indication of what you should be paying per hour.

## Where Should You Look to Find an Extra Set of Hands?

All of this information might sound good, but it doesn't matter if you're unable to find quality candidates in the first place. Luckily, you're not dealing with needing to hire for a position that requires technical skills. This means that looking to people you already know is a great place to start. You already know the positives and negatives of the people you know. You know if you'd work well with them or if they'd get on your nerves. You know if they'd be stubborn and challenge you in every little detail, or if they'd be able to provide valuable feedback to the way things are done. The best approach to this is to think of some people you think would be a good fit to work with, and reach out to them directly and see if they have any interest. You can also post about your opening on your personal social media profiles. Just beware that you may have some people reaching out that you know won't be a good fit, and you'll have to deny them. If you think that's something you'll have a hard time with, then it's best to just message people directly.

If you don't know of anyone you'd work well with, then you're going to have to look elsewhere. A good place to look is online groups. You can specifically look at catering groups, restaurant groups, waiter groups, and other similar groups. These groups will be filled with people who have direct experience doing what you need them to do. And the best part of all of this is that you don't have to resort to a paid method of finding the right candidate, such as advertising on a job board, for example. Job boards are great as you will get flooded with a lot of candidates, but it can get pricey to post your job. I want to give you some other options to consider that will be more budget-friendly for you. So when it comes to posting about your opening, what should you say? Here's a good way to talk about your opening:

"Hello everyone, I'm looking for an extra set of hands to help me out with an upcoming catering gig I have coming up. Previous experience is preferred but not a requirement. I'm estimating that the job will be for about 6 hours on Saturday, March 16th. The pay will be $17 per hour. Please reach out directly or comment below if you have any questions or are interested. I will definitely continue to hire you for future gigs if we're a good fit working with each other. Thank you!"

# Conclusion

This business is rewarding, no doubt about that. There's something so special about getting to see lots of people enjoying food that you prepared all at once. It truly takes a good amount of effort to be able to cater for an event, but the effort is worth the reward. The main thing that will separate a successful catering company from a failing one is sales. That can be the hardest thing for aspiring entrepreneurs to grasp because they just want to focus on the food side of things. After all, you're in the catering business so that mentality makes sense. If you approach things with lead generation first then fulfillment, you will be more successful. Therefore, in the beginning, you need to focus as much attention as you can on generating customers for your company. It will take a lot of hustle in the beginning to get things going, but your company will snowball soon enough. Don't give up when you're going through tough times and nobody is booking. Every action you take matters even if you don't see it. A couple you talked to months ago at a bridal show may suddenly call you. A business you reached out to may suddenly be in need of your service and the only way they knew about you was from an email you sent 3 weeks ago. These are the small things that add up to your success in this industry. You've already shown the initiative by reading this book, so I know that you're capable!